~ *Craft Ideas for Your Home* ~

BED COVERINGS

~Craft Ideas for Your Home~

BED COVERINGS

VICTORIA WALLER

FRIEDMAN/FAIRFAX
PUBLISHERS

To my family and friends, for their endless support, love, and encouragement.

Acknowledgments

*Thank you to the many fine designers and photographers
whose work graces the pages of this book.*

A FRIEDMAN/FAIRFAX BOOK

© 1996 by Michael Friedman Publishing Group, Inc.

All rights reserved. No part of this publication may be reproduced, stored in a retrieval system, or transmitted, in any form
or by any means, electronic, mechanical, photocopying, recording, or otherwise, without prior written permission from the publisher.

Library of Congress Cataloging-in-Publication Data available upon request.

ISBN 1-56799-278-1

Editor: Elizabeth Viscott Sullivan
Art Director: Lynne Yeamans
Photography Editor: Colleen Branigan
Production Associate: Camille Lee

Color separations by Fine Arts Repro House Co., Ltd.
Printed in China by Leefung-Asco Printers Ltd.

For bulk purchases and special sales, please contact:
Friedman/Fairfax Publishers
Attention: Sales Department
15 West 26th Street
New York, New York 10010
212/685-6610 FAX 212/685-1307

Contents

Introduction • 6

EQUIPMENT AND MATERIALS • MEASURING YOUR BED • BED AND BEDDING MEASUREMENTS
PURCHASING AND HANDLING FABRIC • BED COVERING PROJECTS

PART ONE

The Master Suite • 22

PART TWO

Guest Rooms • 46

PART THREE

Theme Decor • 56

SOURCES • *70*
CONVERSION CHART FOR COMMON MEASUREMENTS • *70*
INDEX • *71*

Introduction

The bedroom is an intensely personal room—the place where all days begin and end. This is why it is the ideal setting for total decorating indulgence. The bed, usually the most predominant piece of furniture, can easily become the focal point of the room and the basis upon which the balance of bedroom decorating rests. The bed can be soft and inviting, full of lush pillows and opulent bed coverings, or tailored and serene, creating the perfect retreat from life's hectic pace. A bedroom can be decorated with ready-made ensembles, adorned with a blend of purchased and handmade creations, or personally designed, filled with details that hold special meaning. However you choose to accomplish your decorating vision, the bed is is an excellent place to start.

A bed is often the first item purchased when starting a new home. In days gone by, a bed and a table were the only pieces of furniture in the entire house. The house itself was simply a shelter from the elements; the bed was a mat or cot to rest one's weary head, and comfort was not an option. One-room dwellings were still the norm as late as the 1600s, where the bed, often built into the wall, was shrouded in heavy drapes for privacy and warmth. Wealthy landowners eventually built larger quarters with separate rooms for living and sleeping; however, the bedrooms remained sparsely furnished.

Not until the latter 1600s, with the influence of Louis XIV, did more opulent bedroom furnishings appear. The demand for richly trimmed fabrics and ornately carved furniture increased as the public attempted to imitate the royal court. Armoires and washstands took resi-

Opposite: Architectural molding dramatically frames this peach bed like a giant headboard. In a brilliant strategic play to create depth and intrigue, a scroll-framed tapestry was positioned above the bed. Held aloft by celestial cherubs amid a pattern of suspended ribbons, it appears to be reflecting the room below. Where does the bed end and the wall begin? Closer inspection reveals that these are indeed separate pieces functioning as one, repeating theme and color to double the already impressive impact.

Left: This profusion of print makes a perfect hideaway when tucked into a corner under an eave or stairway. The bed, almost invisible against the draped alcove, is defined only by ecru lace and the green moiré lining of the duvet cover. Lace also trims the leading edge of the drape, pulled aside to expose the table and pictures floating in a sea of pattern.

dence as standard bedroom furnishings. Comfort and style became as essential to bedroom decor as function. Over the centuries, history has combined these three elements, leaving us a rich legacy of decorating options.

Bed accessories, such as soft blankets and lofty pillows, that were once considered a luxury are now taken for granted. Voluminous bed swags, cloistered canopies, and upholstered headboards, originally designed to function as insulation or privacy panels, are updated in our modern bedrooms with contemporary fabrics. Old favorites easily team up with new inspiration to offer today's consumer endless decorating choices.

Bed coverings can range from a simple, textured throw over a stunning antique sleigh bed to tailored spreads and blankets mimicking a western cabin to the sumptuously draped and trimmed damasks and tapestries of a European castle. All these treatments are surprisingly easy to create. With just a few yards of flat fabric or sheets and basic sewing skills, you can create the look of an ivy-covered country cottage, a lace-filled Victorian boudoir, or a fanciful fairy-tale retreat for a child. Cut and sew your fabric or simply drape and tie it together, then embellish with trims and tassels to transform any bedroom from merely ordinary to spectacular.

The instructions and tips that follow offer the basics you'll need to create one-of-a-kind bedroom coverings—decor torn from the pages of history, or treatments that are refreshingly new and unique. Easy techniques for sewing duvet covers, constructing boudoir pillows, or swagging a four-poster bed are clearly illustrated so that you can create an environment that is at once unique and distinctly personal—the bedroom of your dreams.

Equipment and Materials

The bed covering projects in this book require some basic sewing equipment. In addition to fabric, thread, optional trims, and padding, you will need a sewing machine with basic accessories, hand-sewing needles, straight pins, T-pins, a tape measure, a straightedge ruler or yardstick, fabric marking pens, and scissors. Simple projects, such as padding a headboard, may require only a hot-glue gun and glue sticks or a staple gun. For projects requiring some carpentry, such as hanging a drapery rod or canopy, you will also need screwdrivers, hollow wall anchors, and a hand drill. In all cases, a large work surface is very valuable.

Sewing Machine A basic zigzag sewing machine is all that is required. Purchase machine needles size 80(12) for light- to medium-weight projects and 90(14)–100(16) for upholstery-weight fabrics and decorative trims. Use the regular presser foot that comes with the machine for basic sewing. A zipper foot, included with most sewing machines, is invaluable when sewing decorative trims. It is adjustable and allows you to stitch close to the cord or fringe. Your sewing machine may have a seam guide to help you sew a straight line, or you can place a piece of masking tape ½" to the right of the needle. Align the raw edge of the fabric with the masking tape as you sew for perfect ½" seams.

Hand-Sewing Needles Keep handy a package of embroidery or crewel needles in assorted sizes for basting or finishing throw pillows. These needles have a large eye for easy threading.

Pins Straight pins are used to hold fabric pieces together until they are sewn. Long quilting pins with plastic or glass balls covering the heads are best for bulky fabrics or attaching trims when a small, thin pin might get lost. T-pins can temporarily hold fabric and padding to a wood frame or headboard; these pins are strong and easy to see. A magnetic pin holder makes cleaning up annoying pin spills a snap.

Tape Measure and Straightedge Ruler A tape measure is essential for planning fabric projects. One that has measurements on both sides is best. A straightedge ruler or yardstick is helpful when estimating positions of wall treatments or for marking straight lines; an L-shaped ruler aids in marking and cutting square corners.

Fabric Marking Pens Fabric marking pens allow you to mark cutting or fold lines, as well as starting and stopping points for sewing. Some are formulated to disappear with heat or to evaporate after a period of time. Test the pen on a scrap to make sure that no marks are permanently visible on your project.

Scissors Keep two pairs of scissors on hand: large, bent-handled shears for all the fabric and trim cutting, and smaller embroidery scissors for clipping threads or ripping out incorrect stitching. Never use sewing scissors to cut paper or for other household chores.

Iron-On Adhesives These are available in 17"–18" widths or in narrow 3/8"–7/8" strips. Follow package directions for use. Be sure that the "care" instructions of the adhesive are compatible with the fabric or trim being used.

Hot-Glue Gun and Glue Sticks Use these to adhere fabric or trims to padded headboards, cornices, lampshades, and other projects when sewing or iron-on adhesives are not practical.

Staple Gun This is the best tool to use when stretching fabric and padding over a headboard or wooden valance. Usually, 3/16"–3/8" staples work best.

Screwdrivers Phillips and flat-head screwdrivers are used to mount screws into rod brackets or to attach a headboard to a bed frame.

Hollow Wall Anchors Sometimes called Molly screws, these are best for mounting projects to a hollow wall; nails do not hold as well and are not as easy to remove for readjustment.

Hand Drill While most screws can be started with a small nail hole, a hand drill is the most reliable, professional way to prepare a surface. If you have never used one, don't despair. Hand drills are lightweight and easy to handle. Most come with a variety of drill bits.

Seam Ripper To rip out incorrect stitching or to open up a pillow casing, a seam ripper is an indispensable tool that will save you time and frustration.

Introduction

Measuring Your Bed

Whether your plan is to purchase or make your own bed coverings, the first step is always to measure your bed. Measure the width, length, and depth of your undressed mattress to ensure the best-fitting sheets (see diagram below). Some new mattresses have "high-contour" shapes requiring an extra-deep pocket on the side of the fitted sheet. If a water bed is your preference, you may use conventional sheets for a soft-sided bed or purchase water bed sheets from a specialty store for a hard-sided bed. Next, measure your bed with the sheets, blankets, and pillows in place. Extra layers of thick blankets or quilts will increase the bed size. This second set of measurements can be used to create custom bed coverings or to enable you to purchase ready-made items that will fit correctly.

Bed height varies with bed frames, so be sure to include this in your set of measurements. The average height (called the drop) is 19"–22" from the top of the mattress to the floor. Bedspreads usually extend to the floor; bed skirts are designed to fit over the box spring, concealing the bottom half of the bed frame. Comforters and duvet covers, which hang just 10"–12" from the top of the bed, can be used to reveal a peek at a pretty bed skirt or to show off the beautiful wooden frame of a sleigh bed.

Ready-made bed covering sizes are created to fit conventional mattresses but may vary slightly from brand to brand. The "Bed and Bedding Measurements" chart that follows on page 10 lists the finished sizes of basic bed coverings. Compare your own set of measurements to the ready-made product sizes. For instance, if your full-size bed measures 54" wide × 75" long (average), but measures 30" from the mattress top to floor, you will see that your bed is much taller than what is considered average (19"–23"). A standard comforter will drop about 11" on the sides and foot of the bed (there is no drop at the head of the bed), leaving a 19" gap between the floor and comforter. A standard purchased bed skirt would also look skimpy. But if you create your own bed coverings, you can make a larger comforter with an increased drop and a bed skirt that fully covers the remaining space.

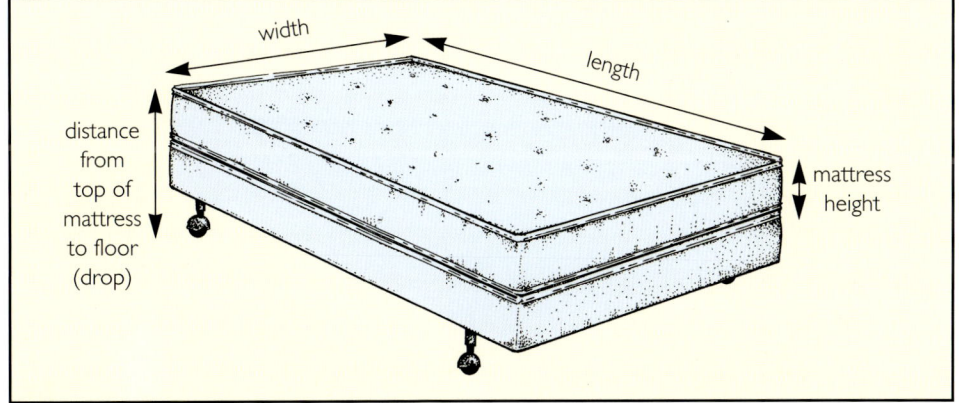

Bed and Bedding Measurements

The "Yardage Requirements" chart on page 11 converts the finished measurements into yardage so that you can calculate the amount of fabric you will need to make your own bed coverings. Most bed coverings require a finished width greater than the width of available fabric, so fabric panels must be pieced. Sheets, however, are never pieced. In fact, it is usually best to purchase sheets and pillowcases ready-made for reasons of economy and comfort. With their high thread count, combed yarns, easy-care permanent finishes, and seamless construction, ready-made sheets provide the ultimate in sleeping comfort.

Yardage Requirements

Fabric choice is a matter of taste, but one that is generally influenced by decorating style. Whether you opt for sheer, gauzy fabric or heavyweight tapestry, always consider how much wear and tear the fabric will be able to endure as well as its care requirements. A daybed that does double duty as an office couch, for example, will need a sturdier, more tightly woven decorator fabric than a daybed in a master bedroom that receives far less traffic. White silk is beautiful, but could be problematic in terms of upkeep, while a cotton damask in a deeper shade will be less demanding. Finally, when purchasing trims and fabrics, be sure durability and care needs are compatible.

Yardage amounts are given in the chart, "Yardage Requirements for Basic Bed Covering Projects," on the opposite page for fabric widths

Bed and Bedding Measurements

	Twin or Daybed	Full (Double)	Queen	King	California King*
Mattress Size	39W × 75L	54W × 75L	60W × 80L	78W × 80L	72W × 84L
Pillow	Standard 20W × 26L	Standard 20W × 26L	Queen 20W × 30L	King 20W × 36L	King 20W × 36L
Flat Sheet	66W × 96L	81W × 96L	90W × 102L	108W × 102L	108W × 102L
Fitted Sheet	39W × 75L	54W × 75L	60W × 80L	78W × 80L	72W × 84L
Bedspread	81W × 110L	96W × 110L	102W × 118L	120W × 118L	114W × 120L
Comforter or Duvet Cover	63W × 86L	76W × 86L	86W × 92L	101W × 92L	92W × 101L
Dust Ruffle	Fits above mattress size; drop of 14"–15" from top of box spring to floor				

The above mattress sizes are a guide only and may vary with manufacturers. All measurements are in inches.
W=Width L=Length

*****California King** is also known as **Western King**. This larger size is not available everywhere.

Introduction

Yardage Requirements for Basic Bed Covering Projects

	Twin or Daybed	**Full (Double)**	**Queen**	**King**	**California King**
Bedspread (Purchase the same amount of lining or backing fabric)	6⅛ yards, 45"–58"W	9¼ yards, 45"W or 6⅛ yards, 54"–58"W	9⅞ yards, 45"W or 6⅝ yards, 54"–58"W	9⅞ yards, 45"W or 6⅝ yards, 54"–58"W	10 yards, 45"W or 6¾ yards, 54"–58"W
Edge Trimming per row	8½ yards	9 yards	9½ yards	10 yards	10 yards
Comforter (Purchase the same amount of lining or backing fabric)	5 yards, 45"–58"W	5 yards, 45"–58"W	5⅛ yards, 45"–58"W	7¾ yards, 45"W or 5⅛ yards, 54"–58"	8⅜ yards, 45"W or 5⅝ yards, 54"–58"W
Edge Trimming per row	8⅜ yards	9⅛ yards	10 yards	10⅞ yards	10⅞ yards
Bed Pillow Sham	1⅝ yards, 45"–58"W per sham	1⅝ yards, 45"–58"W per sham	1⅝ yards, 45"–58"W per sham	1⅝ yards, 45"–58"W per sham	1⅝ yards, 45"–58"W per sham
Edge Trimming per row	3½ yards	3½ yards	3¾ yards	4 yards	4 yards

W=Width

of 45" or 54"–58". The yardage given for decorative trim is for the outer edge only. If decorative trim on inside seams is part of your design, extra trim will be required. To calculate your own trim requirements, measure all the seams you wish to have trimmed. The sum total plus ¼ yard for joining is the required yardage. Remember, it is far better to purchase a little extra trim than to run short; there is nothing more frustrating than finding you don't have the yardage you need midproject.

Purchasing and Handling Fabric

Fabrics with a Large Print or Plaid Before purchasing fabric with a predominant print or plaid, place a second piece of the same fabric against the first. Slide one section against the other as if you were planning a seam; if the printed design blends at the seam line, you will be able to sew your seams without worrying about matching the print. If there is a jarring jump between the printed areas, you may wish to purchase extra fabric so that you can match this design when connecting the panels.

Measure the printed design from its beginning until it repeats again. This distance is called the repeat. Add one repeat for each additional complete length of fabric required. For example, if the fabric you plan to use for a 90"-long comforter has an 18" repeat, the second panel should be 90" + 18" for matching. If a third panel is required, increase the third panel length by 18" to allow for matching the design. To sew a panel that requires matching, place the two pieces right sides up; slide one over the other until the design lines up. Pin to hold, then place the panels right sides together, pinning every few inches to keep the matched sections together. Check the alignment frequently. If the project has a center panel with two side panels, use the center as the one to which the other two must align.

Fabric Grain Line

Most fabric is woven with lengthwise and crosswise threads. The directions of these threads are called the grain lines. The lengthwise grain line runs parallel to the selvage edge (tightly woven finished edge); the crosswise grain runs parallel to the cut edge. For the most professional-looking projects, these grain lines should be perpendicular to one another. To check the grain line of your fabric, simply pull a crosswise thread along the bottom cut edge (or carefully trim the edge along one thread line). Place your fabric on a large table with square corners. The selvage edge should align with one table side and the newly cut edge should align with the adjacent table side forming a square corner. If it does not, the fabric must be pulled into as square a shape as possible. (Another set of hands is helpful here; see diagram below left.) Grasp the short corner, one hand holding the selvage and one holding the cut edge. Have a helper grasp the opposite corner (at the other cut end of your fabric piece). Pull slowly but firmly away from each other, stretching the diagonal grain of the fabric. Place the fabric back on the table to check the corner. If it is still not square, repeat the procedure. Press to remove any wrinkles created.

Bed Covering Projects

Square Fringed Pillow

Materials
1 pillow form, 14" square
½ yard of fabric, 45"–58" wide (58"-wide fabric will make 2 pillows)
1⅝ yards of fringe, 1½" long
Matching thread

Creative suggestion: use a tapestry panel as the pillow front, with velvet or moiré as the pillow back for a rich, vintage effect.

1. Measure the pillow form (A). Cut 2 squares of fabric (one pillow front, one pillow back) to the exact pillow size (B). Trim the corners to prevent a dog-eared shape (C).

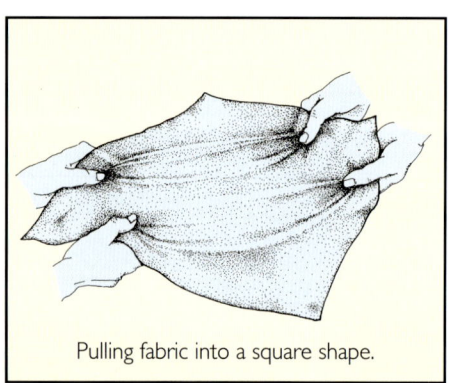
Pulling fabric into a square shape.

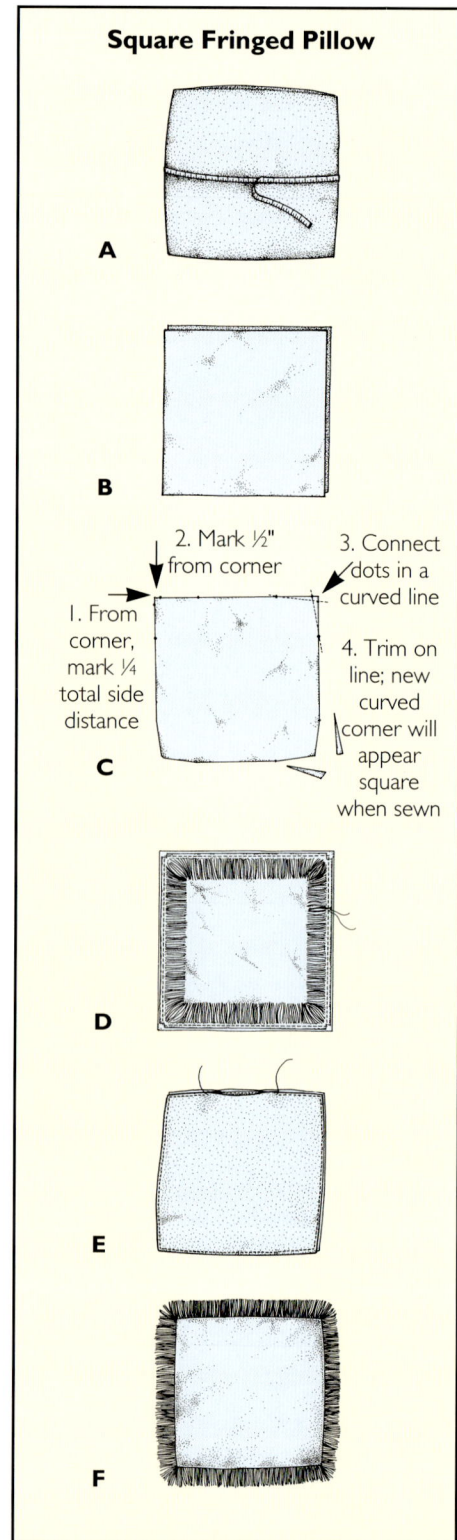

2. Right sides together, stitch the fringe to the front panel. Start at the bottom center edge so that the cut fringe ends point toward the center of the pillow (D). Use a zipper foot to stitch along the innermost row of fringe stitching. Clip this row of stitching at each corner. Butt the fringe ends together to finish; do not overlap.

3. Pin the pillow back to the front, right sides together. Stitch together, leaving 8" unstitched on one side to turn (E). Turn right side out; press.

4. Insert the pillow form; slip stitch closed (F). If your fringe has a protective row of stitching along the cut ends, remove it now. Steam the fringe ends to fluff.

Boudoir Pillow

Materials
1 pillow form, 12" × 16"
⅝ yard of fabric, 45"–58" wide
¾ yard of tassel fringe
1⅞ yards of cord-edge, ³⁄₁₆"–⅜" diameter
Matching thread

Note: measurements are given for the exact placement of inner seams, but you can also design your own one-of-a-kind pillow pattern.

1. Follow the instructions in Step 1 of "Square Fringed Pillow" (page 12), substituting paper for fabric. Use this pattern to cut one piece of fabric for the pillow back; set aside. Use the paper pattern to create the pillow front: measure in and draw a line 4½" from, and parallel to, each short side of the paper pattern (A). Cut on the lines. Add a ½" seam allowance to each new cut edge (B). Pin each pattern piece

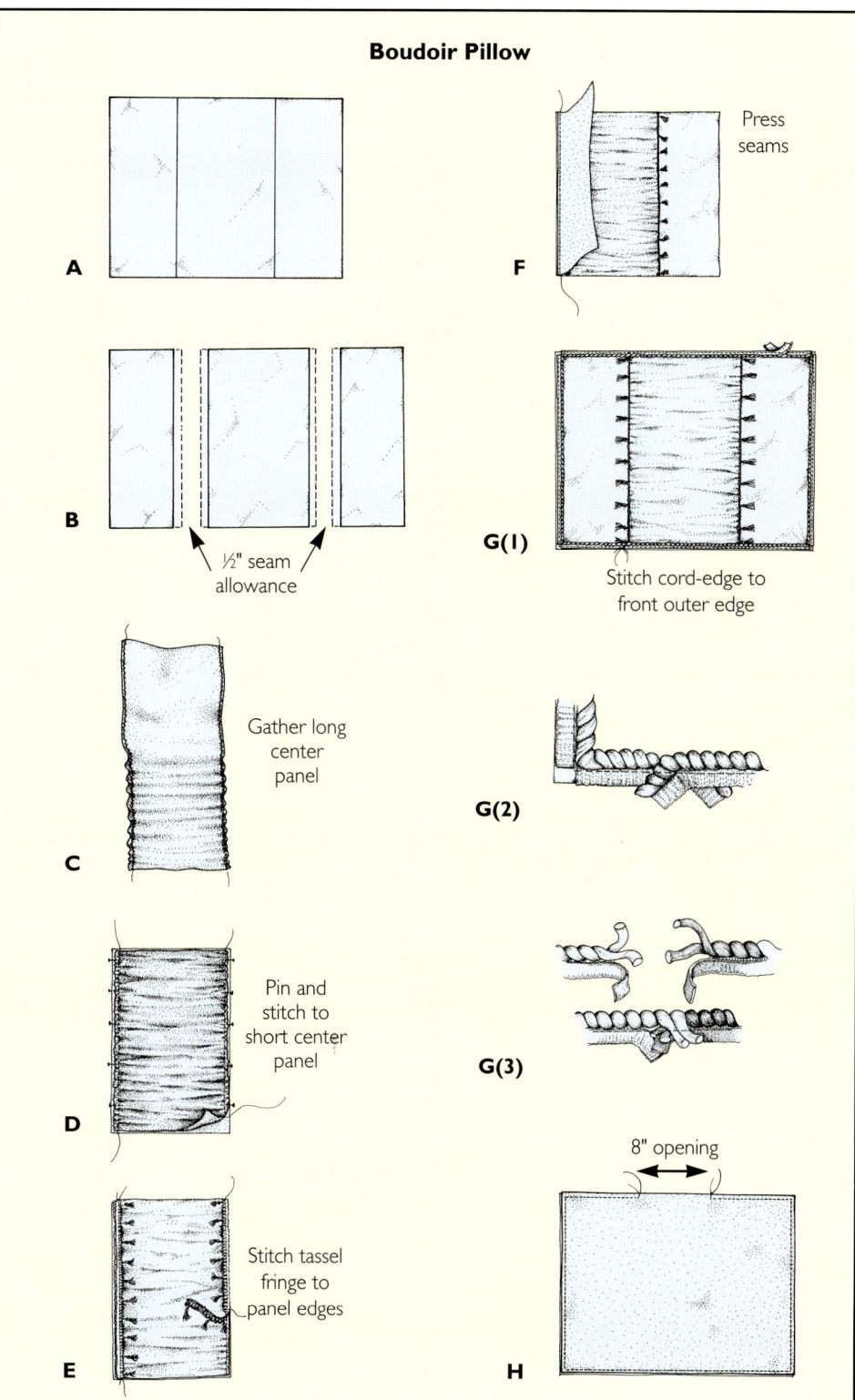

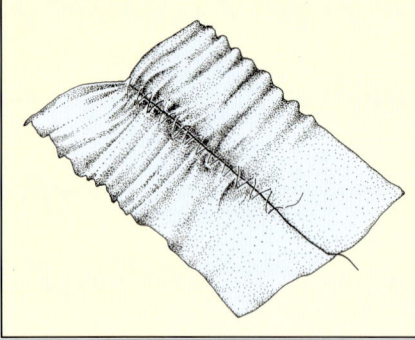

To gather without frustrating thread breakage, place a piece of thin cord on the ½" seam line; stitch over the cord with a zigzag stitch so that the needle does not catch the cord. Pull the cord to gather the fabric.

to the fabric so that the straight edges align with the straight fabric grain; cut. Cut another fabric strip that is the exact width and 2½ times the length of the center fabric panel.

2. Gather the long edges of the long center panel (C) as described in the sidebar above. Pin the gathered strip to the short center panel, easing the gathers to fit (D). Straight stitch around the gathered strip to secure.

3. Stitch the tassel fringe to the gathered panel edges, right sides together (E); use a zipper foot to stitch on the seam line flush to the inside trim edge. Pin the side panels to the center panel right sides together; stitch (F). Press the seams toward the sides.

4. Stitch the cord-edge to the front outer edge with a zipper foot (G1). Start at the center bottom edge, leaving a 3" cord tail. Stitch with a zipper foot on the inside edge close to the cord, stopping within 2" of the corner. Raise the zipper foot; clip the flat trim edge at the corner to the inside row of stitching. Stitch to the corner; pivot with the needle in the fabric. To ensure a sharp corner, place your left thumb against the cord corner before lowering the foot; push the cord gently away from you. Lower the foot and continue around, repeating this procedure at each corner. Return to the beginning. Clip excess cord so that you end with a 3" tail. For ³⁄₁₆" cord-edge, overlap the tails in the seam allowance and stitch over the cords to finish (G2). For ⅜" cord, clip the chain stitch, attaching the cord to the gimp in the tail section only. Separate the cord from the gimp; untwist and overlap the cord ends so that the cord plies are parallel (G3).

5. Pin the back to the front. Stitch around, leaving an 8" opening on one side to turn (H). Turn right side out; press edges. Insert pillow form; slip stitch closed.

Duvet Cover with Cord-Trimmed Edges

Materials

Fabric: See "Yardage Requirements" (page 11) for amount.

Lining or backing: Use matching or contrasting fabric in the same amount as for the duvet top (face).

Matching thread

Cord-edge (twisted cord with a gimp edge attached for seam insertion): See "Yardage Requirements" (page 11) for amount.

Velcro® hook and loop fastener: 7½" length for twin- and full-size; 10½" length for queen- and king-size. (Ribbon ties or buttons may be substituted for Velcro.)

Old comforter, for filling duvet cover

1. Measure your bed and prepare your fabric following the "Bed and Bedding Measurements" chart (page 10) and "Yardage Requirements" (page 11). The top of your duvet cover, called the face, will be prepared first. Divide the finished duvet width by the fabric width to determine the number of fabric lengths you will need to cut. Any fraction will become a whole length. (Example: Your double duvet width is 76". Divide 76" by 45" [fabric width]. The result is 1.69 or 2 complete fabric lengths. A king-size duvet [101" wide] when divided by 45" will yield 2.24 or 3 fabric lengths.) These panels of fabric will be pieced together. When two lengths are required, one length will be the center panel, and the other will be split lengthwise to create one narrow panel for each side. A center seam is never used. Wider duvets will have a full panel on each side of the center.

2. Cut your fabric into the number of equal fabric lengths required. Pin one side panel to each long edge of the center panel, right sides together; stitch (A). Press the seams open flat (B).

3. To adjust the cut size of your duvet, fold the pieced fabric in half lengthwise, aligning the seams. Mark a line parallel to the fold line, measuring ½ the finished width plus 1" seam and ease. Cut on the marked line (C). Repeat for the length, folding crosswise and measuring ½ the finished length plus 1" seam and ease. The bottom corner may be cut into a curve by using a round plate. Use the plate as a guide; trace and cut on traced line (C).

4. *Cord-edge:* follow Step 4 of "Boudoir Pillow" (page 14) to attach cord-edge to the duvet face (D). Start at the top center edge; pin the trim in place in 4" sections on one side at a

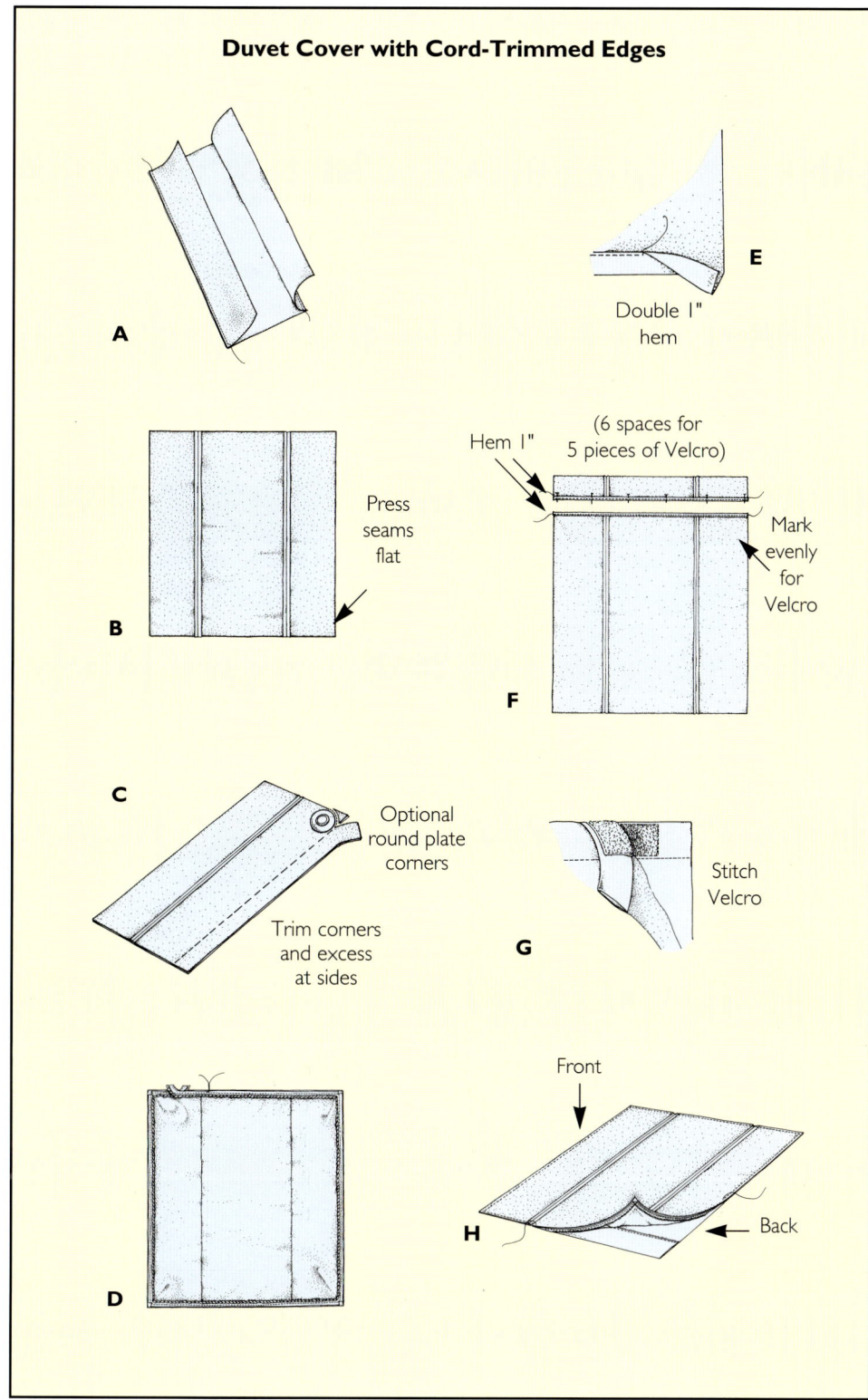

time only. Use a zipper foot to sew closely to the cord. Keep the cord relaxed as you sew; never pull.

5. *Duvet back:* cut the backing fabric panels each 6" longer than the face panels. Stitch together and press as in Step 2 (page 14). Adjust the width as in Step 3 (page 14). Measure and mark a line 12½" down from, and parallel to, the top cut edge. Cut on this line. Fold the new cut edge of each piece 1" to the wrong side twice for a double 1" hem (E); pin. Press; edge stitch close to hem edge. *Top section:* divide the width into even sections (6 for twin- or full-size, 8 for queen- or king-size). Place a pin at each point for Velcro placement (F). Overlap the hemmed edge of the top and bottom back duvet, right sides up, aligning side cut edges; pin. Transfer Velcro markings to bottom section. Cut Velcro into 1½"-long strips. Pin the corresponding Velcro strips to the markings on each section. Stitch in place around the outer Velcro edges (G). Overlap duvet sections; seal Velcro. Follow Step 3 (page 14) to adjust the duvet back length.

6. The duvet back should match front in size. (If you have pulled the cord-edge while sewing the front, it may be slightly smaller; ease the back to the front. If the size difference is great, you may have to remove and adjust the cord-edge.) Pin the back to the front. Stitch from the back side along the ½" seam line with a zipper foot (H). Clip the fabric at corners to remove bulk. Turn right side out; press edges flat. Slip the old comforter inside the new duvet cover.

Comforter

Materials

Fabric and lining: See "Duvet Cover" (page 14).
Decorative trim (welt, cord-edge, or fringe): See "Yardage Requirements" (page 11) for amount.
Matching thread
High-loft polyester fiberfill batting, cut to desired size

1. Follow Steps 1, 2, and 3 of "Duvet Cover" (page 14). Cut the back panels the same size as the front panels. Stitch the back pieces together and press as in Step 1 of "Duvet Cover."

2. Position the comforter face on the batting, wrong side down. Secure with pins placed every 4" around the cut edges. Machine or hand baste the comforter edge, removing all pins as you stitch (A).

3. Attach the trim to the edge of the comforter face (B). Pin the comforter back to the front, right sides together. Stitch around, leaving 18" unstitched along the top edge to turn (C). Turn right side out; press edges. Pin the 18" opening closed; slip stitch.

4. Working on a large flat surface, pin the back to the front across the comforter at even intervals. *Pad stitch in one of the following ways. Tuft:* stitch and knot yarn or sew small buttons at evenly marked intervals (D). *Parallel rows of machine quilting:* baste comforter through all thicknesses. Tightly roll up the part of the comforter that is not in work. Ease the pinned layers through your sewing machine, stitching rows parallel to the comforter edge (E). Check the underside periodically to prevent pleating. *Motif quilting:* handle comforter as for parallel rows. Straight stitch around printed designs across the comforter face (F).

Pillow Sham

Materials:

Fabric and trim: See "Yardage Requirements" (page 11) for amounts.
Matching thread

1. Measure your bed pillow. *Front:* Cut one fabric piece to the pillow size plus 4½" all around. *Back:* cut 2 back panels, each to the measured pillow height plus 9", and ½ the pillow width plus 9". *Optional:* stitch cord or welt to the front edge.

2. Hem the inside vertical back edge: press one short edge of each back fabric piece 2½" to the wrong side. Press the cut edges under ½"; stitch close to the folded hem edge (A). Overlap the back sections until the finished size matches

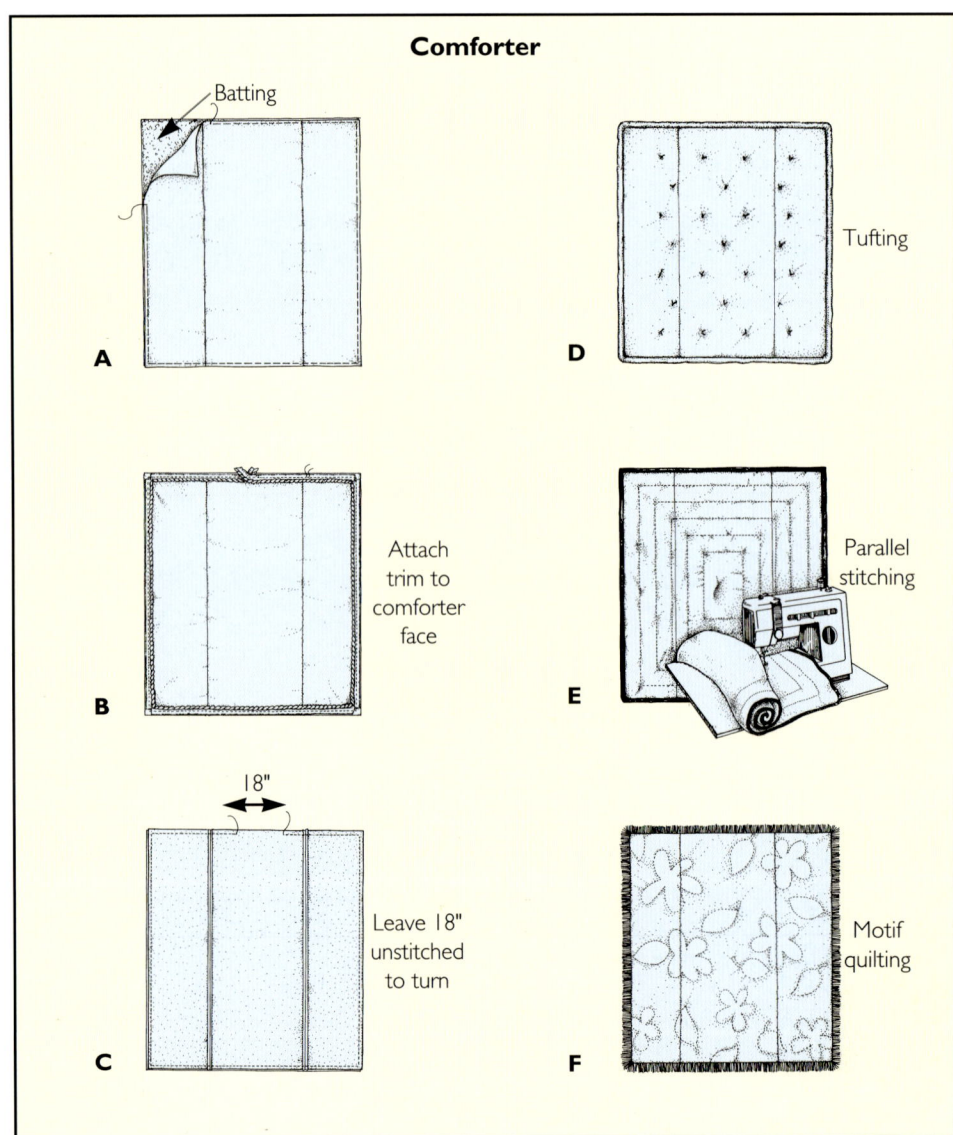

Introduction

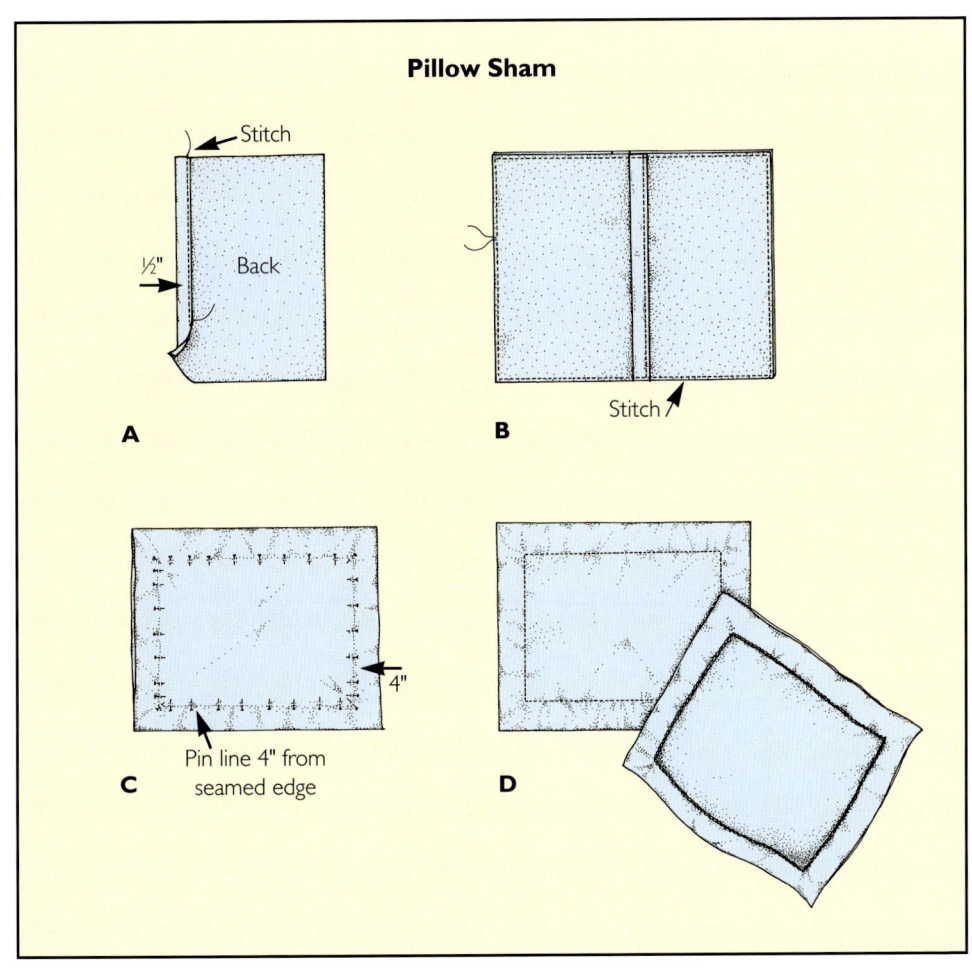

1. Measure the headboard height (not including the legs), width, and depth; then measure the height and circumference of the headboard legs if you would like to cover them with fabric (A). Determine the dimensions of the fabric and batting pieces you will need: height + (2 × depth) + 10" = required fabric and batting length; width + (2 × depth) + 10" = required fabric and batting width. You may find that the finished fabric width may require piecing. Divide the required width by the fabric width to determine the number of fabric lengths you will need to purchase. You may wish to add ½ yard to your measurements to cover the headboard legs, or you can cut these covers from fabric scraps (see Step 2, this page). Then follow Steps 1 and 2 of "Duvet Cover" (page 14) to cut and piece the fabric panels. To adjust the finished fabric width, fold the pieced fabric in half lengthwise, making sure to align the seams. Mark a line parallel to the fold line, measuring ½ the required finished cut width; cut on this line. Cut the batting to match the fabric size.

2. If your comforter or bed skirt does not hide the headboard legs, you may wish to cover them with fabric. For each leg cover, cut one piece of fabric to these dimensions: (leg height + 2") long × (leg circumference + 1") wide. Press the bottom cut edge under 1" and one side edge under ½" to the wrong side. Place the fabric lengthwise so that it covers one front leg with the unpressed vertical fabric edge extending ½" toward the inside of the leg. Pierce with 2–3 T-pins to hold. Staple the ½" extension to the inside leg at 3" intervals (B). Wrap the fabric snugly around the leg; clip the top edge at corners, if necessary. Overlap the ½" extension; staple the pressed vertical edge in place so that the

the front panel. Pin; baste the top and bottom edges along the overlapped hems (B).

3. Place the front and back right sides together. Pin; stitch together.

4. Turn right side out; press. Measure and place a pin line 4" from each seamed edge (C). Stitch along the pin line through all thicknesses, creating a 4" flange (D). Remove the pins as you stitch; press. Insert the pillow through the back opening.

Optional: stitch braid to the front pillow sham, covering the row of stitching.

Padded Headboard

Covering and padding the headboard of a bed is an excellent way to transform a marred or out-of-fashion wooden bed into a thing of beauty. The outside shape should be smooth—curved or square, with no knobs or design protrusions. You may wish to purchase a padded headboard kit (available in some fabric stores), or you can create your own following these instructions.

Materials
Fabric: See Step 1, this page.
Thick polyester fiberfill batting: See Step 1, this page.

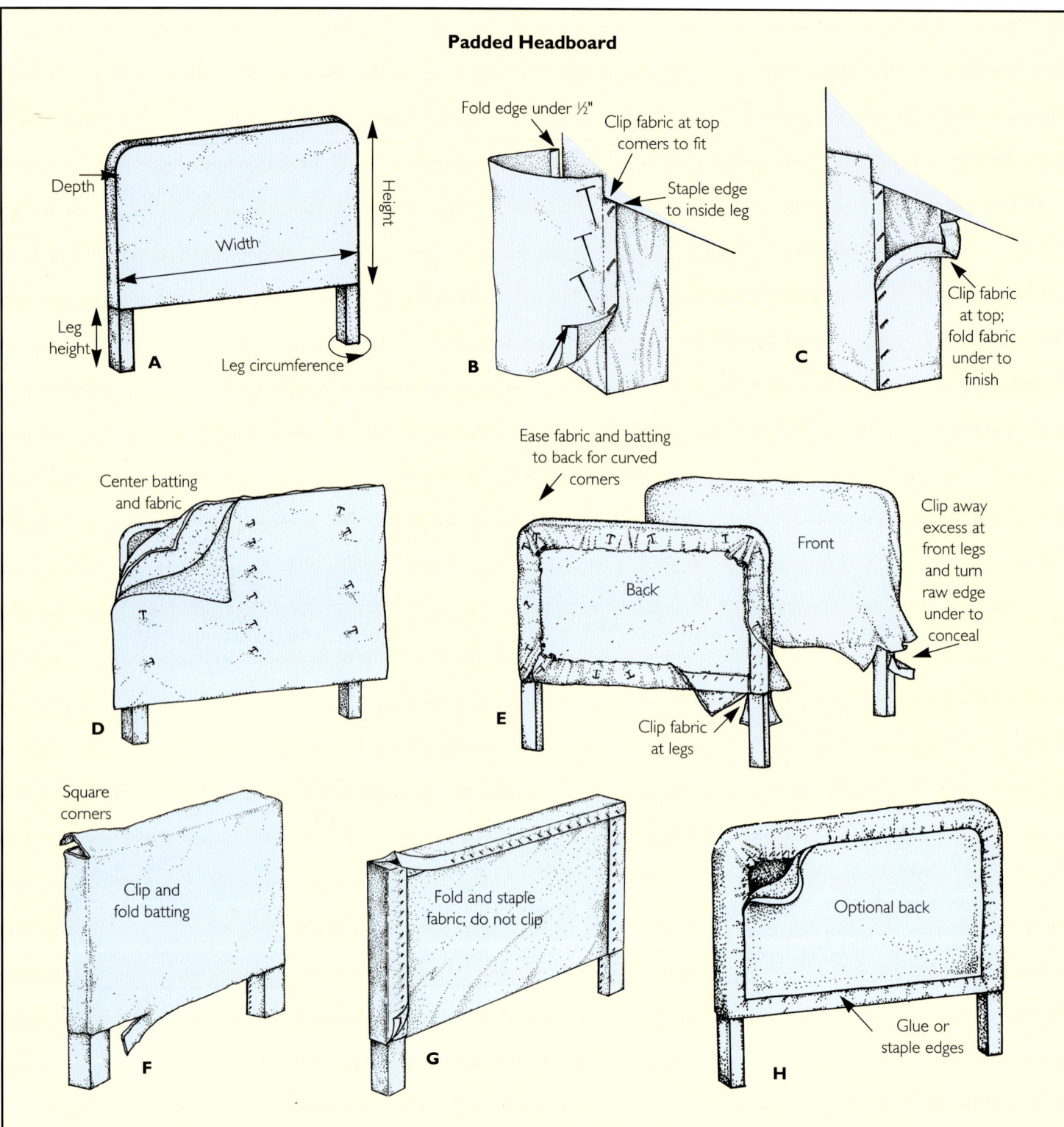

fold is flush to the leg edge (C). Repeat for the second leg.

3. Center the batting across the headboard front. Pierce it with T-pins along the center to hold (D). Stretch the batting slightly to each side; secure with pins. Stretch the batting evenly between the top, bottom, and side pins. *For a curved shape:* pull the batting around to the back of the headboard so that there are no puckers; secure with pins (E). *For square corners:* clip the batting at each top corner so that it folds flat (F). Staple the batting in position to the headboard back. Clip and trim the batting around each leg in a line even with the bottom of the headboard. Add a second layer, if desired, for extra fullness.

4. Center the fabric across the length and width of the headboard, stretching it to fit as with the batting. Secure with T-pins until the fabric is even and smooth across the front. *For a curved shape:* pull the fabric smoothly to the back with no wrinkles. *For square corners:* fold the fabric under at each top corner so that the fold is flush to the headboard edge. Pull the fabric smoothly to the headboard back; staple in place (G). Clip the fabric at the intersection of the leg and the headboard, folding the cut edge so that it covers the top edge of the leg fabric.

5. *Optional back cover:* If the back surface of the headboard will be visible, cover it with an additional piece of fabric. Measure, cut, and piece the fabric as in Steps 1–2 of "Duvet Cover" (page 14). Cut the fabric to the outer headboard dimensions. Press the cut edges under. Pin in place so that all raw fabric edges are covered, then staple or glue the folded edge in place (H).

Draped Four-Poster Bed

This fully dressed look requires an enormous amount of fabric. You may choose to decorate on a budget by shortening the floor length tails to short top tails only.

Materials
Fabric: See Step 1, pages 19–20.
Trim: See Step 1, pages 19–20.
Matching thread
Scrap cord for hidden ties

1. *Cutting and preparing swags and floor length tails* (See C): add the following measurments: the top frame perimeter × 1½ plus the bed post height top to floor × 8, plus 8 yards for swagging and hems. (This may require as

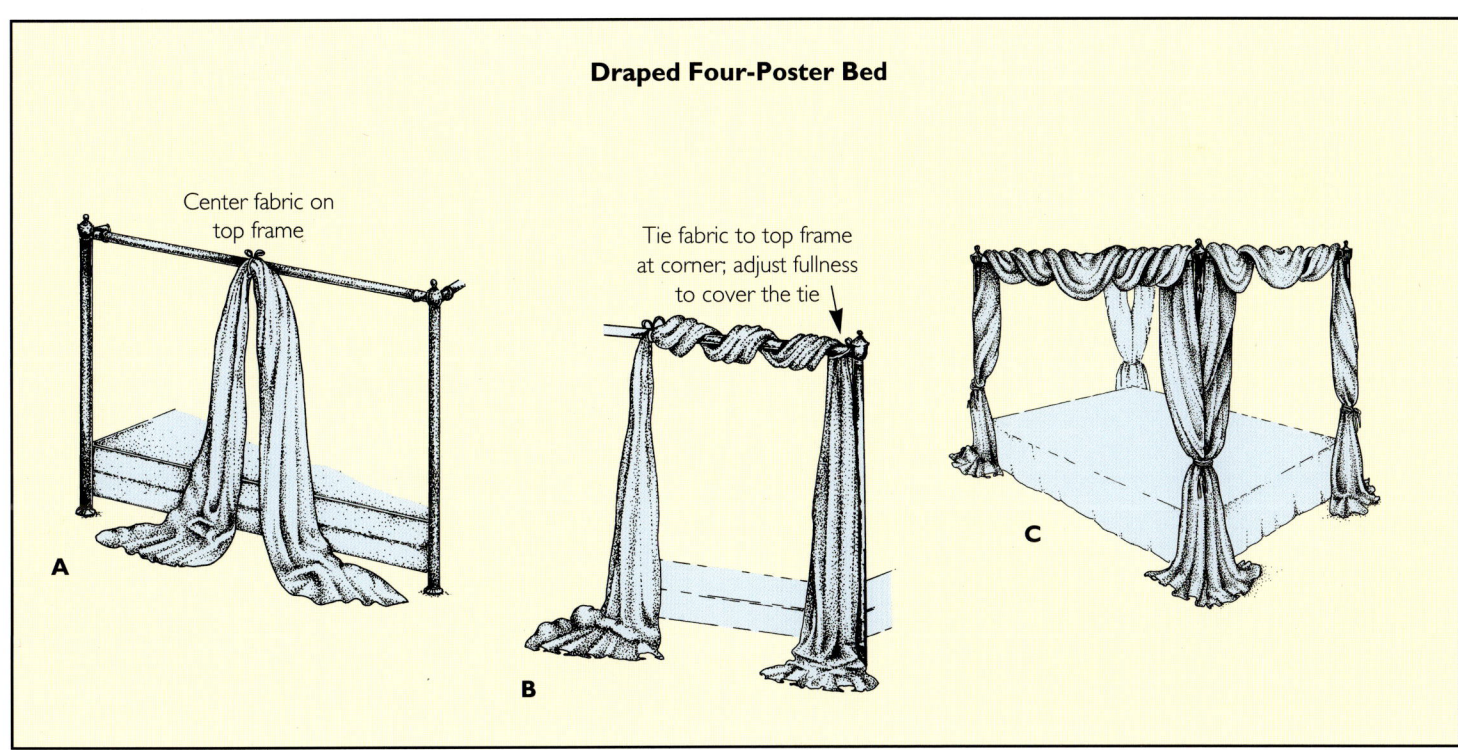

Draped Four-Poster Bed

Center fabric on top frame

A

Tie fabric to top frame at corner; adjust fullness to cover the tie

B

C

much as 20–35 yards to complete. To decrease yardage, divide the total measurement in half. Then split the purchased fabric in half, lengthwise. There will be one half the fullness all around, but will cost half as much.) *To purchase trim* (C): to attach trim along one edge only, the trim yardage will equal the fabric yardage. A simpler version would have trim on the leading (inside) edge of the tails only; yardage would equal that of the total post height plus 4 yards.

2. *Side bed panels:* add together: (1½ bed lengths) + (2 × height) + (2 yards). Cut 2 pieces of fabric to this measurement. *End bed panels:* add together: (1½ bed widths) + (2 × height) + (2 yards). Cut 2 fabric pieces to this measurement.

3. Test the wrap first to ensure correct length, then hem and rehang permanently. First, fold one side piece in half crosswise. Tie or tape the center point to the center side top bed frame (A). Loosely wrap, right side out (B), toward one end bedpost. Repeat from the center point, working in the opposite direction. Repeat for the remaining sides of the bed.

4. *Finishing:* the bottom tail edge can either be hemmed in double 1½" hems or trimmed with tassel fringe. The vertical edges can either be hemmed in double 1" hems or trimmed in tassel fringe. To sew tassel fringe, follow Step 3 of "Boudoir Pillow" (page 14). Stitch with tassels pointing toward the center of the fabric. Ease the trim to the fabric to avoid puckering.

5. Tie the fabric to the top frame at each end. Floor length tails can puddle slightly or can be pulled to the side and tied to the bedpost with tasseled tiebacks. You may wish to hand tack the fabric at the top corners to keep it in the desired position (C).

Introduction

Simple Half Canopy

Materials

Fabric: See Step 1, below.

Lining: See Step 1, below.

Long fringe: See Step 1, below.

Matching thread

2 drapery poles, 1½" diameter (the length should equal the width of the bed)

2 sets of brackets (or large hooks to securely hold drapery poles)

1. The total fabric length will be the distance from the wall pole to the floor, plus 56½". The width of the canopy will be the same as for the bed, plus two double 1" side hems (A). Divide the bed width by the width of the fabric to determine the number of fabric lengths required. (See "Duvet Cover," page 14.) *Lining:* cut length is 55½"; width is the same as the canopy. Only the top and front drop are lined. The lining is pieced to match the canopy fabric. Fringe yardage is equal to the width of the canopy plus 4" for ease.

2. Mount the drapery poles on the ceiling centered across the bed width so that one pole is flush to the wall and the other is 24" from the wall.

3. One fabric length will be the center panel and the remaining fabric will be divided evenly on each side as in the "Duvet Cover" instructions. Stitch side panels to the center panel, right sides together. Repeat this step for the lining fabric.

4. Mark each long edge of the canopy fabric at 16½", 19", 52½", and 55" from the front corners (B). On the right side of the fabric, connect corresponding marks with a fabric marking pen for rod pocket placement.

5. Clip the fabric edge in 2" at each 55" mark (C). Press a double 1" hem from the clip to the bottom cut edge. Machine stitch side hems in place. Press a double 2" hem on the bottom cut edge; stitch. Trim 1½" from each side of the remaining canopy fabric, from the clip at the 55" mark to the top cut edge (D).

6. Stitch the fringe to the front cut edge (D) as described in Step 2 of "Square Fringed Pillow" (page 13). Stitch right sides together. Ease fringe to fit; do not pull.

7. Pin the lining to the canopy section of fabric with right sides together. Trim the lining edges 1½" to fit the trimmed canopy (D). Press the cut edge of the lining under ½" at the 55" line. Stitch along sides and front end only, leaving the space between lines unstitched for rod pockets (E). Turn the canopy right side out. Press flat.

8. Lay the canopy flat. Pin through both thicknesses at the rod lines. Stitch on marked lines, removing pins as you stitch (F).

9. Insert draping poles through pockets to hang fabric (G).

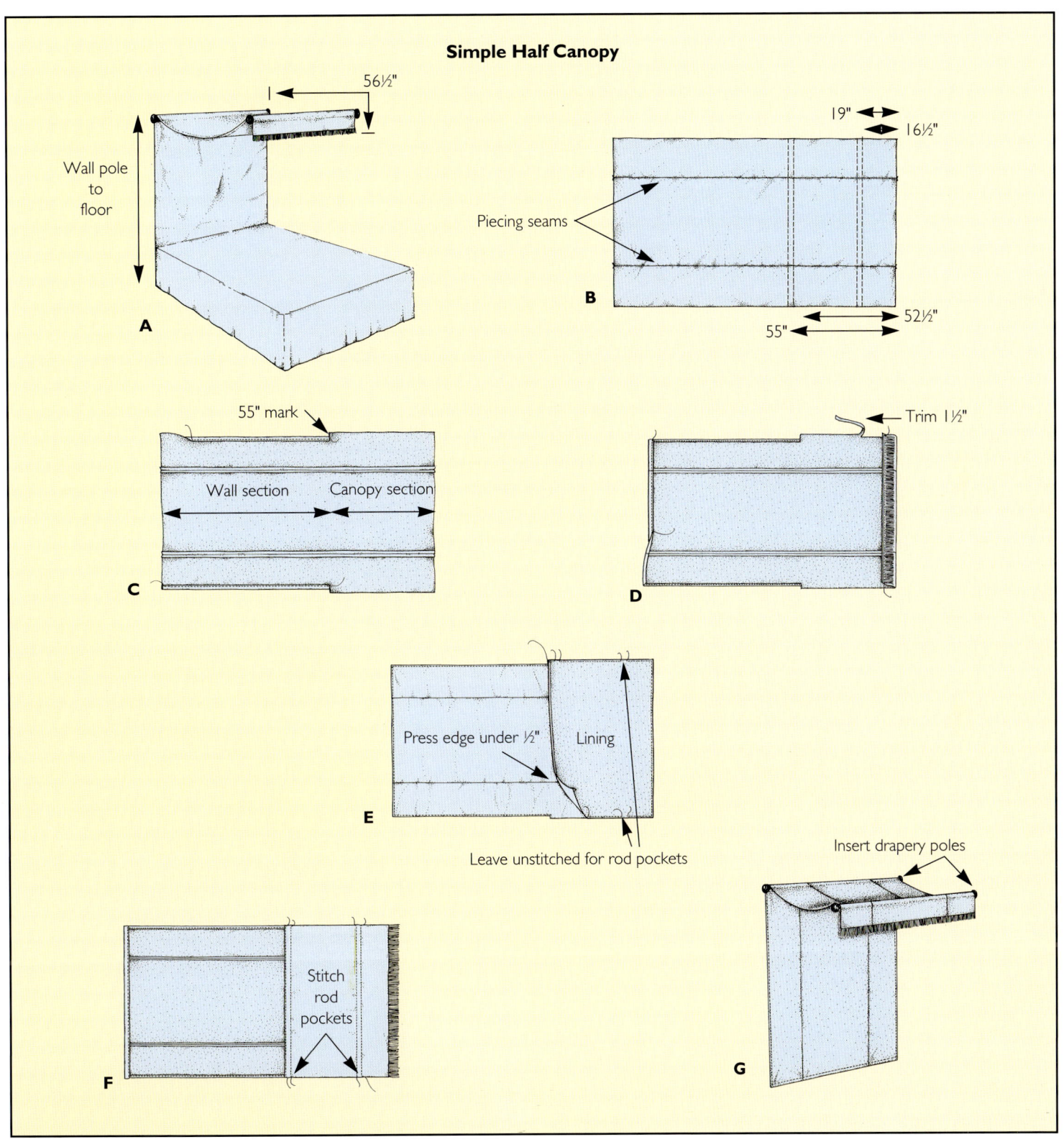

PART ONE

The Master Suite

*E*nter the master suite—spacious, open, often with an adjoining sitting area. Designed to reflect your personal style and taste, this room can be the most unique in the home. A master bedroom can be functional, utilizing tailored bed covers and crisp sheeting, or wildly indulgent, with layers of down comforters, and floral bouquets adorning the bed and walls alike.

Where do you begin to create a room that will reflect your personal style and meet your design requirements? Choosing a general theme, such as western, Victorian, or contemporary, is often a good way to start. Think of the mood you would like the room to suggest. A casual, masculine atmosphere can be expressed in a western theme, for example, fashioned in shades of tan, red, and navy or dark green. Victorian decor, often sultry in nature, can achieve its feminine goal with shades of pink and wine. If you are not sure about a motif, start by picking a color scheme. Color can set the mood, create the illusion of space, or envelop you in shades of sensuous seclusion. You can then repeat basic design elements in your bed coverings and coordinated accessories to reinforce the theme, to create flow or focal emphasis while achieving your decorating vision.

The photographs that follow depict a range of bed coverings, from simple airy linen covers to tailored spreads and blankets to sumptuously draped and trimmed damasks and tapestries. In each idea-filled photograph you will see how the bed coverings set the tone for the entire bedroom, dictating other fabric and color choices, the accessories, and the overall theme. Look closely and you will also see how small details— tasseled and trimmed accessories, for instance, or the repeat of a design element such as a scalloped bed-skirt edge that mirrors the scallops on a wrought-iron bed frame—can transform an ordinary bedroom into the ultimate master suite.

*O*pposite: *Reminiscent of a simpler time, this shining brass bed is dressed in its Sunday best. The iron bars of the bed and the edging on the lace bedspread echo the arched corner motifs on the painted ceiling. The heavy detail on the propped-up bed pillows emphasizes the floral-printed carpet below and the soft, painted detail above. Wrapped with a frieze of swirling scrollwork, this Victorian boudoir evokes memories of private, proper afternoon teas.*

*L*eft: *This simple iron bed offers no interference for the display of freshly pressed white linens. The airy display of pillows is in perfect contrast to the black iron bed frame and allows the best of each element to be revealed.*

The Master Suite

Opposite: A web of knotted and tasseled lace, this artful canopy exposes the structural ribs of the bed framework to keep the eye aloft and create an illusion of height. Patterns visually link this turn-of-the-century room together—the canopy to the quilt, the wallpaper to the carpet. The tasseled fringe is repeated on the edges of the traditional cotton bedspread and window treatments. An antique hope chest displays and repeats the curved patterns so strongly defined by the arched bed frame above.

Above: Yards of lace trail gently to the floor from this gracefully curved iron bed that crowns at the top. The elegant structure holds the eye within its framework, and releases it only to view the hand-painted flowers that cascade across the ceiling to the floral-patterned window dressing below.

Right: Decor is kept low-key in this small but well-lit room. A four-poster bed is topped with a richly edged Battenburg lace canopy that sags softly at the center, repeating the swagged and knotted window treatments on wide-open double-hung windows. A rest in this shadowy retreat provides gentle transport to years gone by.

The Master Suite

The Master Suite

Opposite: Rich yellow and teal fabric flow from this regal crown that drapes like a cape across the shoulders of the luxurious bed that rests below. Note how the lighter yellow bed receives extra attention against the teal backdrop. A repetition of key details—bed covers edged in white to match the wall molding, bed pillows scalloped to match the crown—helps to unify this well-ordered bedroom.

Above: The flatness of this crisp white bed cover stands out in stark contrast to the cascades of white fabric falling lightly from the ceiling. Topped with an identical valance, this draped wall accentuates the height of the room while drawing attention to the bed itself. A table cover of white cutwork lace adds to the airy effect. This lightness might be overdone if it were not for the heavier box-pleated bed skirt and armchair, which are used to balance to entire room.

The Master Suite

Above: Cool white blends with the most subtle shades of gray for a simple, sophisticated effect. Crisp white covers and lace-trimmed pillows float like clouds on a pale gray sky. The white bars of the bed frame hold the gathered fabric at bay, softly diffusing light to complete the effect of this soothing gray and white environment.

Opposite: In this window-lined room, one panel of panes has been whited out with paint, leaving only one window open to serve its original intent. The harshness of the white light is tamed here by subtle fawn-toned patterns covering the bed clothes. Lace trims on the bed coverings soften the effect of the repetitious conservatory-style windows.

The Master Suite

The Master Suite

The Master Suite

Left: In this environment of contrasts—steel and wood, cool and warm, hard and soft—all opposing elements are integrated by matching fabric. The diffused light of floor-to-ceiling windows casts a sheen across the floor to give the impression that the bed is floating—an apparition of stripes and sculpted framework fading into the light beyond.

Below: A gracefully curved bed breathes softness into a hard-edged room. Lace bed coverings dress up the serene, sophisticated setting of linear walls and striped upholstery.

Opposite: Breakfast is served in the master suite. A painted checkerboard floor helps to frame this large room, setting the tone for its blue-on-white palette. An upholstered cornice and a backdrop of shirred fabric make the white-covered bed a haven of calm in the busy surroundings.

The Master Suite

Opposite: A whimsically scalloped sleigh bed stands in dark relief in this sunny bedroom. The closed-in nature of the bed and the tossed bedding of garden-fresh colors give the room a cozy friendliness and charm. The bed skirt, placed so that it does not conceal the beautifully shaped bed frame, hangs below. A delicate, fagoted border appears to float at the skirt's edge, which repeats the flanged borders of the pillows.

Above: The three pillars of this bed frame extend just above the green ribbon-print bed dressings. Scalloped bedspread edges are softly repeated in the cream bed skirt and pillow flanges. The placement of the dark wool blanket adds solidity and intensifies the greens and creams.

The Master Suite

34

The Master Suite

Opposite: The wall behind this bed was draped in white to showcase the ornate wrought-iron bed frame, which otherwise would have been lost against the dark wood wall. The contrasting theme was continued to the bed itself so that the frame would stand silhouetted in full glory against the white coverlets. Colorful accent pillows glow like gemstones set into filigreed jewelry.

Above: Chocolate brown and sage green are not colors normally associated with whimsy. But with ironwork and spotted dogs guarding this bed and ornamental plaster tassels and bows adorning it, the mood in this bedroom is hardly somber. The brown, when used in temperance, is not overwhelming, especially when surrounded by layers of gauzy fabrics to filter light and soften the earth tones.

Left: An art wire chair stands poised to dance beside this delightfully appointed bed. White-on-white trapunto surface detail stands strong against the blue and white quilt pattern. Sharp angles take center stage in this strongly stylized setting.

The Master Suite

Left: A lacy, gilded window offers the inspiration for this lofty, feminine room. Simple bed coverings of pink and white complete the decor. A gold-crowned standing mirror reflects the elegance of the space.

Opposite: Extremely high ceilings with both high and low windows provide excellent accommodations for this massive bed. Small in its other dimensions, the room has ample flow when the bed is turned at an angle. Natural fabric is twisted like a carelessly flung scarf atop the tall four-poster bed. The frame is left open on top to allow light to shine in from above.

Right: This room is kept deliberately simple to maximize the beauty of the seaside vista. The sleigh bed, dramatic and powerful, needs no accompaniment. Ruffled bed coverings lend a feminine air; a casually draped fringed blanket adds warmth on crisp nights.

The Master Suite

The Master Suite

The Master Suite

Above: Embroidered organdy in shades of blue and orange are perfectly suited to the orange-highlighted floral inlays of this ebony bed. As in this setting, such a whimsical piece can become part of an eclectic decorating scheme, where each element, so different from those around it, shines in unique glory.

Left: This antique bed, created centuries ago, is not only narrower than today's double bed, but is shorter as well. The framed four-poster has been left undraped to retain the open atmosphere. Wall sconces and an antique tapestry mounted high ensure that the eye will not remain at bed level. Warmed by shades of butterscotch and caramel yet sparkling with white floral highlights, this bedroom exudes a humble earthbound quality and is firmly rooted in history.

The Master Suite

Opposite: Stripes and checks are geometrically linked throughout this roomy composition. Rafters are exposed to repeat the parallel lines and soaring height of the impressive bed frame. The simplicity of the bed coverings allows the architectural framework to dominate. With its flared, winglike draperies, this white-clad bed seems ready to take flight.

Above: The inconspicuous wire frame extending from this bed exists solely to support the cascading fabric. These bed drapes are tied tightly at the top corners, creating ruffled fabric rosettes; the fabric then falls into soft puddles on a large, round-cornered carpet. Recurring stripes and medallions repeat throughout for cohesive decorative impact.

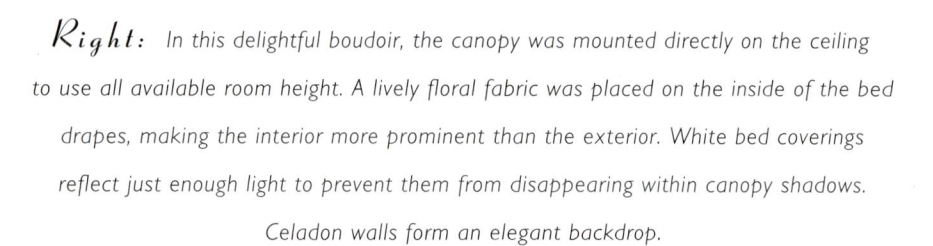

Right: In this delightful boudoir, the canopy was mounted directly on the ceiling to use all available room height. A lively floral fabric was placed on the inside of the bed drapes, making the interior more prominent than the exterior. White bed coverings reflect just enough light to prevent them from disappearing within canopy shadows. Celadon walls form an elegant backdrop.

41

42

The Master Suite

Opposite: This tall four-poster bed has been painted and draped in patina green to create a tented, ornate appearance. Both bawdy and kitsch, this setting serves up showmanship with a wink. Yellow satin tufted upholstery, velvet chairs, and mural-painted screens complete the carnival atmosphere.

Above: A regal red velvet bed sits at the center of this impressive master suite like an island unto itself. Notches created by the pleated fringed canopy are repeated in the simpler gold-bordered bedspread, just as the clublike crowns topping each bedpost are duplicated in the exaggerated carpet corners. The interior has been lined in a more humble overall print, permitting the majestic fleur-de-lis to dominate the exterior coverings.

The Master Suite

Opposite: Silk drapes the bedside tables as well as the bed and walls in this Victorian-inspired bedroom. Luscious embroidery, silk, and ribbons—all interpreted in shades of ecru and white—grace the edges of the bed and table covers alike. These same colors and details are used to tie this boudoir seamlessly to the adjacent room. The Victorian lampshade adds whimsy and personality to the beautiful setting.

Above: Modern style and simplicity of design describe these inlaid furnishings. The checkerboard bed is positioned atop a raised section of floor against a geometric backdrop of windowpanes. Each piece of furniture and each pillow are strategically placed throughout the room.

Right: Accessories cannot compete with this dramatic, ornate brass bed. Soft flowing layers of sheer fabric and white-on-white detailing create frothy bed coverings that blend, but don't compete, with their surroundings. Even the bedside chair fades into the room, allowing the bed its full measure of attention.

The Master Suite

SARGENT
OLSON
JULIA MORGAN, ARCHITECT
O California!
GIORGIO ARMANI
EGON SCHIELE
WATERCOLORS AND DRAWINGS
ROMANCE
TAJ MAHAL
BRANCUSI

PART TWO

Guest Rooms

When guests converge upon your home, there is no greater relief or joy than to have the perfect room for their stay. Decorating a guest room can be rewarding and fun. Usually smaller than the master bedroom, a guest room requires less furniture, takes less wear and tear, and can double as an office or den. Perhaps it is time to create such a useful, welcoming room in your own home. So why not finish the attic you have been meaning to decorate, or re-do the children's rooms now that they have grown and left home? Converting wasted dormer space into a cozy alcove or closing in an unused porch can also offer valuable guest quarters.

Decorating principles, such as the repetition of and emphasis on certain themes and colors, are just as important here as with master suite decorating. However, because the guest room is an extra room of sorts, decor can be a little more unpredictable, including daybeds and window seats, lively colors, and arrangements of unusual collections. To that end, the rooms that follow offer creative, innovative suggestions.

~

Opposite: The morning star alights and the sun streams in, putting louvered shadows into play across this guest room. The sueded walls and furnishings mute the boundaries between light and dark, soft and hard. Softly curved pillow sham edges, suggesting neither feminine flounce nor hard masculine border, merely enhance the play of shadow across line and form.

~

Left: A vanilla-wrapped single bed has been tucked into the window alcove of this utility office to increase sleeping space. Waves of scallop-edged pillows—crisscrossed with middy-braid and delicately appliquéd with white flowers—rest against the padded headboard. To make the bed cover less tailored, a wavy construction seam was used to repeat the scallop theme and lessen the squareness of the plain foot of the bed.

Guest Rooms

Opposite: The striped floor in this guest room keeps the angled walls from closing in as it increases the spaciousness and helps to separate furnishings of such disparate nature. The gold-colored bed skirt involves the bed in the actual structure of the room, surrounding it in the glow of the faux-finished walls. The softly printed bed covers keep the bed surface from becoming too bland, yet drape it in extreme simplicity.

Above: This sunny guest room is simple in form, almost cubic in execution. Pink pillows line up for inspection on a custom bed cover seamed to carry on the square theme. Clay tiles and a woven leather-strapped bench bring the soaring colors back to earth, all the while echoing the square geometry.

Right: Hidden beneath this tented canopy, one can recline in privacy to retreat from daytime stress or to rest as a weary nighttime guest. Structural lines and subtle shadows set the tone here as the sculpted golden wood of the Renaissance-inspired daybed is highlighted by the rich striped golds and browns of the cascading fabric. Pillows echo the subtle striped detail, with stripes placed at angles to add interest. The chair and prints reiterate the architectural intent.

Guest Rooms

Guest Rooms

Guest Rooms

Opposite: Such a multitude of red patterns could make a room too busy. But when layered in profusion, these red prints almost cancel one another out, creating an overall backdrop in which larger shapes come to the forefront. The symmetry of the tented bed and accessories repeat the sameness, achieving a calmness in spite of the abundance of high-energy red.

Below: Flawless composition is achieved when all elements are balanced—each accessory positioned just so. Like the framed prints, all the pieces of this composition—the light and dark, the square and round, the curved and straight lines—reside in perfect harmony.

Above: A Native American dreamscape surveys this built-in sofa bed and its updated version of the roped and tied decor. Contemporary stripes and borders repeat paneling lines. Shades of brown and blue reflect the colors of the earth and sky, while towering sunflowers add a burst of natural, vibrant detail.

Guest Rooms

Left, top: Friendly shapes, curvy and welcoming, present a spare yet country-comfortable ambience. Vintage bark-cloth draperies were given a new life as bed coverings, contributing to the aged patina of this room—a welcome retreat for any guest.

Left, bottom: An interplay of stripes and patterns adds lively movement to this functional apartment bedroom. Pillows of various shapes and sizes increase the interest of the pattern-on-pattern display. The creamy yellow tones of the comforter add warmth to the slate blue details. Sunny flowers add a welcoming touch.

Opposite: This room is spare on furniture, but not on charm. Pillows that are seemingly carelessly tossed have appeal when they share a common design theme. Floppy flange borders differ only in the size and shape of the scallops, creating a cohesive blue and white decorative look.

Guest Rooms

Guest Rooms

Opposite: Delicate embroidery and cutwork-covered pillows sit in soft repose, creating no interference with the multicolored wedding ring quilts they adorn. This bed treatment sits like the photograph hanging above it—a moment captured from a time when life was simple and the day was well spent.

Below: Stripes give the angled walls of this top-floor bedroom movement, allowing them to recede rather than to crowd the guest bed. Cheerful stars and stripes in primary colors outfit the bed in country charm. Tucked-in bed covers allow the chambray skirt to show, with smaller prints falling back so that the colorful, bolder quilts and pineapple bed frame can take center stage. The red rocking chair is a nice accent, as it makes the room sparkle.

Above: A collection of vintage prints covers these same-size pillows in this homey guest room. The uniformity of pillow size and the similarity of print achieve overall harmony, much like the quilt cover on which they rest. Smaller, more boldly printed pillows are set front and center.

55

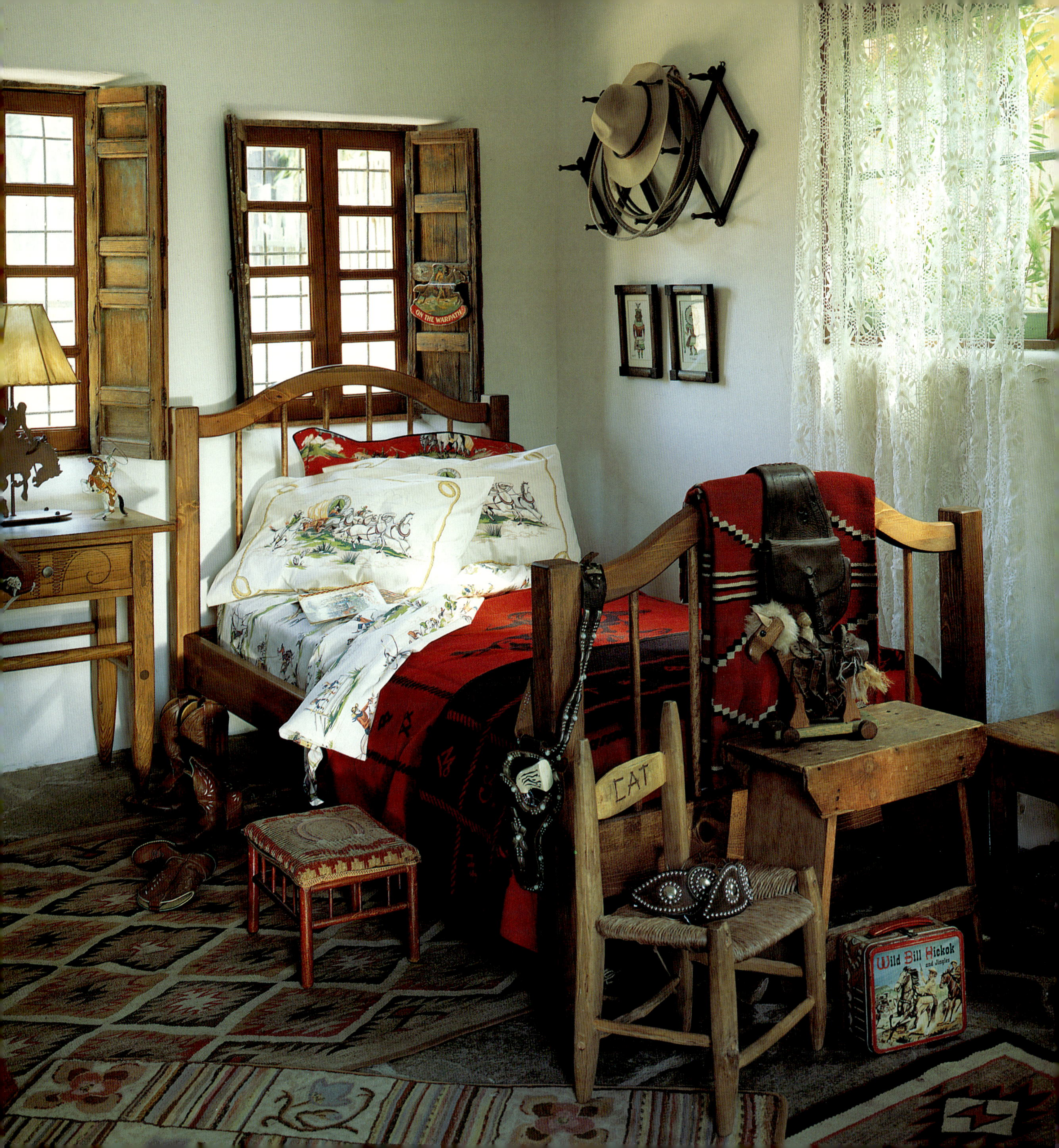
ON THE WARPATH
CAT
Wild Bill Hickok
and Jingles

PART THREE

Theme Decor

All good decorating has a connecting thread—similar elements that link parts of the room to one another. An overall decorating theme, however, when chosen and planned in advance, is not just good decorating; it is theater. It creates the stage upon which individual elements—the bed, bed dressings, and accessories—function like actors in a play. They must interact effectively, not just to create overall ambience, but to tell a story.

Choosing a theme for bedroom decor provides you with a starting point and presents a decorating challenge as well. Perfect accents must have more than visual appeal; they must eloquently speak of the theme at hand. Take, for example, the antique trunk which traveled to the West full of family necessities, resting at the foot of a rough-hewn bent-sapling bed. The trunk's contents are spilled across the room—family portraits, Grandma's log-cabin quilt, a fireplace and iron fashioned as a lamp base. All are necessities turned treasures that tell a rich tale of frontier life. To link these story elements together decoratively, colors and designs are repeated within the collection, reinforcing the storyline and creating a flow throughout the decor.

Inspect the following photographs for the stories they have to tell. Discover the connecting thread that binds the elements of each room together. Hopefully, you will be inspired to tell a story of your own.

~

Opposite: Designed for a bronco-busting eight-year-old or for a guest who appreciates the best of the West, this simple ranch bedroom invites Wild Bill Hickok to ride again. A horseshoe-embellished footstool stands ready to help a young cowpoke enjoy sweet dreams. Weathered shutters, placed on the inside of each window, carry the colorful bunkhouse theme from bed to wall.

~

Left: This Colorado cabin retains the spirit of the mountainous West in which it resides. Chamois pillows bring western lore to life with painted Native American scenes of battles won and coups counted. A staghorn lamp and laced cowhide accessories survive as relics of a time when humans and animals roamed free. The sturdy furniture and rust-red earth tones remind us that nature is the only constant in this mountain environment.

Theme Decor

Left: No bed is perfectly pressed and made forever. This rumpled collection of bedding glows in golden light, creating a friendly, lively atmosphere. A stairstep quilt hangs from bentwood saplings as if to protect the sleeper from the rays of the early morning sun.

Opposite: It would indeed be difficult to find focus in this busy, textural room were it not for the flagpole-mounted fabric and the dazzle of the gold-printed bed covers. A sun motif flashes throughout in pillow designs as well as statuary, while a lesser theme of square design covers the walls and room screen. The total effect is one of shimmering, sunburst elegance.

Right: Given a room where the waterbed filled every available inch and uneven windows dominated the architecture, this designer worked with available resources to create an eclectic room with style and western whimsy. The calla lily–patterned lace hung at the windows actually emphasizes their differences in size. Panels were cut from one large piece, creating details that are similar but distinctive, just like the bed pillows below. Rust curtains and walls mirror the pillow colors, pulling all the disparate elements together. Beads and hat edging accent the pillow patterns for a special touch.

59

Theme Decor

Theme Decor

Opposite: This Eastern-inspired room features secondary themes of color and shape. Gold medallions embellish both the furnishings displayed on the ebony sleigh bed and the walls. Red details trim the elaborate pillows to enhance the sense of ancient, opulent grandeur. A great wall of faux-finished gold guards these spoils of wealth.

Below: Red is the color of unquestioned power in this awe-inspiring decor. Green, the complement to red, helps to neutralize the dramatic red bed, with its cascading ribbons colorfully echoing the lines of the intricately carved chair. Replete with ornate appliqué and positioned strategically to enhance its natural sleigh shape, the bed sits with dynastic dignity as if poised to set sail on the China Sea.

Above: Bordered panels of fabric surround the bed and fall softly from the ceiling, repeating the carpet and wall molding borders in this subtle room. The ceiling panel is set away from the wall, pushing the wall back and emphasizing the bed itself. Simplicity of form and attention to detail make the gold-toned elements of this room a powerful match for the rest of the decor.

Theme Decor

Opposite: The green-lined canopy of this inviting, cavernous bed seemingly expands the bed's height, while the striped chaise positioned at the foot increases the perception of its length. The bed, formally symmetrical by nature and design, is given a slightly offhand attitude by the asymmetrical curve of the chaise. Textural pillows designed in coordinated fabric colors lean casually against the chaise arm, assuring that the planned formality is not so imposing after all.

Above: In this dimly lit room, it is easy to imagine oneself sitting on a log cabin porch gazing at the nightscape beyond. Well-spaced wall stripes that mimic the bed striping add width and height. The beautiful ivory lace bedspread lightens and lends relief to this bold interior.

Theme Decor

Theme Decor

Theme Decor

Opposite: Occasionally a piece of furniture is of such import that it becomes the theme itself. This imposing bed, with its intricate scalloping, rules this room with supreme majesty. The bed wears its intricate canopy like a carved crown—mirrored below in the red-bordered eighteenth-century print fabric. The scallops, so artfully created, are captured and toned down in the bedside wingback chair.

Below: A quilt so sublimely exquisite as this print-bordered example should remain the sole recipient of attention. Here it sits as a testament to the time and effort spent in its creation. Filmy drapes soften the dark bedposts without obscuring the hand-quilted bed cover beneath. A red overall print pillow, quite similar in color and value to the quilt border, makes a perfect accent.

Above: The four posts and heavily carved mantle of this canopy bed would dwarf most bedrooms and all accessories within. Here, the bed not only sits within the scale of this large room, but is also enhanced by the wide wall molding and an oriental rug of grand proportions. Wrapped in mustard velvet skirts, necklaced with beaded fringe, and covered with a white lace bedspread, the bed retains its elegant, old-fashioned, Victorian heritage.

Theme Decor

Left: A small leopard "fez," its jaunty tassel flopped forward, leads an army of Turkish printed pillows that nestle behind the large roll of this buttoned duvet cover. The headboard acts like another rust- and brown-toned print, balancing the rumpled chintz cover at the foot of the bed. Clusters of tasseled chair ties hang from the bedposts.

Right: In an analogous color scheme, the colors used in this room fall side by side on the color wheel. The result is a soft, pleasing color progression—one which could easily happen by the benevolence of Mother Nature. Here, apricot faux finishing provides a sun-kissed backdrop for a red-printed ensemble. This red and peach scheme requires no contrast; accents are provided by the lush green landscape visible beyond.

Theme Decor

Theme Decor

Theme Decor

Left: Decorative swirls and brass appointments accented with gentle ecru lace fill this sun-dappled room. Print-on-print designs present a fresh, feminine approach.

Below: Comfort is the theme here. A padded headboard has been fashioned by suspending a button-tufted cushion with fabric tabs from a brass drapery rod. Layers of matching bed pillows rest against the inviting back support. Reading lamps placed at the sides make the quilted arrangement quite functional.

Opposite: A monotone blending of patterns makes this room work, but the actual theme is floral. The white crocheted bedspread covers the bed like a field of white daisies, making it seem larger. Yellow, pink, and white floral pillow panels accent this garden, emphasizing the trail of yellow petals printed on the fabric of the bed dressing.

Sources

Materials and Supplies

Fabric, thread, and decorative trims for bed coverings are available at local fabric stores as well as by mail. Consult a telephone directory under *Fabric* or *Home Decor* to find neighborhood sources, and check advertisements in home decorating and sewing magazines for mail-order sources. Unusual fabric and trims normally available through the "trade only" may be sourced through interior designers or decorator outlets. Also visit antique stores and flea markets when searching for vintage fabrics and accessories. Often an old pair of draperies offers the perfect yardage for a bed cover with forties or fifties flavor. Accessories, such as Battenburg lace, premade comforters, and decorator pillows, can be found in fabric stores or in bed, bath, and home furnishing stores.

Decorative rods and finials can be found at fabric shops, mass retailers, or home improvement centers. To find lumber and hardware for wall- or ceiling-mounted canopies, visit a lumber yard or home improvement center.

General sewing and craft supplies, such as scissors, needles, pins, glue, and sewing machines, are sold both at fabric stores and through many mass merchants.

Design Ideas

The myriad of home decorating magazines on the market offers a wide range of creative ideas. Visiting decorator showcases in your area is another way to review new design ideas. Home furnishing mail-order catalogs have wonderful suggestions, too. Home sewing pattern companies offer patterns that are often strikingly similar to a treatment you might like to try; with a little inspiration and modification, you can achieve the look you're after.

Save your favorite design ideas in an "idea file" for reference later; that way, you'll always have a little bit of inspiration on hand.

Reading

Consult a newsstand, fabric store, or public library for books and articles on bed decor. General decorating books and books emphasizing decorating with fabric also offer a multitude of ideas and tips. Listed below are six books that provide ideas and technical help beyond the scope of this book.

Brown, Gail. *Slipcovers and Bedspreads*. Menlo Park, Calif.: Lane Publishing, 1979.

———. *Instant Interiors*. Menlo Park, Calif.: Open Chain Publishing, 1992.

Frankel, Candie. *Pillowmaking*. New York: Little, Brown and Company, 1993.

Hirschman, Jessica Elin. *Bedrooms*. New York: Little, Brown and Company, 1993.

Lang, Donna, and Lucretia Robertson. *Decorating with Fabric*. New York: Clarkson N. Potter, Inc., 1986.

Paine, Melanie. *Fabric Magic*. New York: Pantheon Books, 1987.

Conversion Chart for Common Measurements

The following chart lists the approximate metric equivalents of inch measurements up to 20", rounded for practical use. To calculate equivalents not listed, multiply the number of inches by 2.54cm. To convert 36", for example, multiply 36 times 2.54, for an equivalent of 91.44cm, or 91.5cm when rounded.

½" = 1.3cm	
1" = 2.5cm	11" = 28cm
2" = 5cm	12" = 30.5cm
3" = 7.5cm	13" = 33cm
4" = 10cm	14" = 35.5cm
5" = 12.5cm	15" = 38cm
6" = 15cm	16" = 40.5cm
7" = 18cm	17" = 43cm
8" = 20.5cm	18" = 45.5cm
9" = 23cm	19" = 48cm
10" = 25.5cm	20" = 51cm

Index

Alcoves, 47, *47*
Antiques, 39, *39*
Armoires, 7

Bedposts, 28, *28*, 43, *43*
Bedrooms
　guest, 47–56
　master, 23–46
Beds
　antique, 39, *39*
　brass, 22, 23, 44, *44*
　built-in, 51, *51*
　canopied, 8, 20, *21*, 24, *24*, 25, 40, *40*, 43, *43*, 48, *48*, 62, *63*, *64*, 65, *65*
　cornices, 30, 31
　crowns, 24, *24*, *26*, *27*, 43, *43*
　curved, 31, *31*
　drapes, 19, *19*, 20, 28, *28*, 40, *40*, *41*, *42*, 43
　ebony, 39, *39*, 60, *61*
　four-poster, 19, *19*, 20, 24, *24*, 36, *37*, 39, *39*, 42, 43, 65, *65*
　frames, 32, *33*
　headboards, 8, 17, *18*, 19, 47, *47*, 69, *69*
　height, 9
　history, 7–8
　iron, 23, *23*, 24, *24*
　pineapple, 54, *54*
　skirts, 9, 27, *27*, 32, *32*, *33*, 48, *49*, 54, *54*
　sleigh, 8, 32, *33*, 36, *36*, 60, *61*, *61*
　sofa, 51, *51*
　tented, 42, 43, 48, *48*, 50, 51
　wrought-iron, *34*, 35
Bedspreads, 8, 9, 43, *43*
　crocheted, 68, *69*
　edge trimming, 11
　fabric requirements, 11
　lace, 22, 23, 62, *62*, 65, *65*
　measuring, 10
　scalloped, 32, *32*
　tasseled, 24, *25*
Blankets, 8

　fringed, 36, *36*
Boudoir Pillow, 13–14, *13*
Box springs, 9

Canopies, 8, 20, *21*, 24, *25*, 40, *40*, 43, *43*, 48, *48*, 62, *63*, *64*, 65, *65*
　lace, 24, *24*
Ceilings
　exposed rafters, 40, *41*
　high, 36, *37*
Chairs, 27, *27*, 48, *48*
　rocking, 54, *54*
　tasseled, 66, *66*
　tufted, 42, 43
　upholstered, 42, 43
　wire, 35, *35*
Chaise lounges, 62, *63*
Colors, 23, 27, 51, *51*, 57, *57*
　analagous, 66, *66*
　complementary, 61, *61*
　coordinating, 62, *63*
　monochromatic, 68, 69
　primary, 54, *54*
　progression of, 66, *66*
　subtle, 28, *28*
　white-on-white, 35, *35*, 44, *44*
Comforters, 9, 16, *16*
　edge trimming, 11
　fabric requirements, 11
　measuring, 10
Cornices, 30, 31
Coverings, 7, 8
　lace, 28, *29*, 31, *31*
　layered, *50*, 51
　print, 32, *32*, *18*, *19*
　ruffled, 36, *36*
　tucked-in, 54, *54*
　white, 40, *40*
Coverlets, *34*, 35

Daybeds, 48, *48*
Designs
　checkered, 40, *41*, 44, *44*
　fleur-de-lis, 43, *43*
　floral, 39, *39*, 40, *40*, 68, 69

　geometric, 40, *41*, 48, *48*
　patterned, *50*, 51, 52, *52*
　print, 43, *43*, 48, *49*, 66, *66*
　print-on-print, 69, *69*
　stripes, 40, *41*, 48, *48*, *49*, 51, *51*, 52, *52*, 54, *54*, 62, *62*
　symmetrical, 62, *63*
Dormers, 47
Drapes
　bed, 28, *28*, 40, *40*, *41*, *42*, 43
　edging, 7, *7*
　vintage, 52, *52*
Dust ruffles, measuring, 10
Duvet covers, 7, *7*, 9, 66, *66*
　measuring, 10
Duvet Cover with Cord-Trimmed Edges, 14–15, *15*

Fabric(s), 7
　appliquéd, 47, *47*, 61, *61*
　Battenburg lace, 24, *24*
　care needs, 10
　chambray, 54, *54*
　chintz, 66, *66*
　cotton, 10, 24, 28, *28*
　damask, 8, 10
　durability, 10
　embroidered, 39, *39*, 44, *45*, 54, *55*
　floral, 40, *40*
　gathering, 14
　gauzy, 35, *35*
　grain line, 12
　handling, 11–12
　lace, 7, 22, 23, 24, *24*, 25, 62, *62*, 65, *65*, 69, *69*
　measuring, 10
　organdy, 39, *39*
　panels, 61, *61*
　purchasing, 11–12
　satin, 42, 43
　sheer, 44, *44*
　shirred, 30, *31*
　silk, 10, 44, *45*
　velvet, 43, *43*, 65, *65*
　vintage, 64, *65*

Footstools, 56, *57*
Furnishings, 7, 60, *61*, 64, *65*
　suede, 46, *47*
Headboards
　padded, 17, *18*, 19, 47, *47*, 69, *69*
　upholstered, 8

Lace, 7
Lamps
　reading, 69, *69*
　staghorn, 57, *57*
Lampshades, 44, *45*
Linens, 23, *23*

Mattresses
　high-contour, 9
　measuring, 9
Molding, architectural, 6, 7

Pillows, 8, 28, *28*, 44, *44*, 52, *52*
　accent, *34*, 35
　boudoir, 13, *13*
　braided, 47, *47*
　chamois, 57, *57*
　common theme, 52, *53*
　cutwork, 54, *55*
　edge trimming, 11
　fabric requirements, 11
　flanges, 32, *32*, *33*, 52, *53*
　floral, 68, *69*
　fringed, 12–13, *12*
　instructions for, 12, *12*
　lace-trimmed, 28, *28*
　measurements for, 10
　printed, 66, *66*
　same-size, 54, *54*
　scalloped, 47, *47*, 52, *53*
　shams, 16–17, *17*, 46, *47*
　striped, 48, *48*
　textural, 62, *63*
Porches, 47
Projects
　Boudoir Pillow, 13, *13*
　Comforter, 16, *16*

71

Index

Draped Four-Poster Bed, 19, *19*, 20
Duvet Cover with Cord-Trimmed Edges, 14–15, *15*
equipment, 8
materials, 8–9
measuring for, 9–11
Padded Headboard, 17, *18*, 19
Pillow Sham, 16–17, *17*
Simple Half Canopy, 20, *21*
Square Fringed Pillow, 12–13, *12*

Quilts, 54, *54*, 65, *65*
  stairstep, 58, *58*
  wedding ring, 54, *55*

Repeat, 11
Rosettes, 40, *40*

Sconces, wall, 39, *39*
Screens, painted, 42, *43*
Shams, 16–17, *17*
  edging, 46, *47*
  fabric requirements, 11
Sheets, 10
Shutters, 56, *57*
Skirts, 9, 27, *27*, 32, *32*, *33*, 48, *49*, 54, *54*
Square Fringed Pillow, 12–13, *12*
Styles
  contemporary, 23, 44, *44*
  country, 8, 52, *52*, 54, *54*
  Eastern, 60, 61

eclectic, 39, *39*, 58, *58*
formal, 62, *63*
Native American, 51, *51*, 57, *57*
Renaissance, 48, *48*
Victorian, 8, *22*, 23, 44, *45*, 65, *65*
Western, 8, 23, 56, *57*, *57*, 58, *58*
Swags, 8

Tables
  bedside, 44, *45*
  covers, 27, *27*
Tapestries, 6, 7, 8, 39, *39*
Tassels, 13
Themes. *See* Styles.
Throws, 8
Trapunto, 35, *35*

Walls
  angled, 54, *54*
  draped, 27, *27*, *34*, *35*, 44, *45*
  striped, 62, *62*
  sueded, *46*, 47
Washstands, 7
Waterbeds, 58, *58*
Windows, 44, *44*
  alcoves, 47, *47*
  conservatory-style, 28, *29*
  floor-to-ceiling, 31, *31*
  gilded, 36, *36*
  swagged, 24, *24*
  tasseled, 24, *25*
  uneven, 58, *58*

Photography Credits

FRONT COVER PHOTOGRAPHY: © WILLIAM ABRANOWICZ, Stylist: Christopher Hersheimer
BACK COVER PHOTOGRAPHY: © TIM STREET-PORTER, Designers: Debra Jones (top left), Robert Woolf (bottom left); © WILLIAM ABRANOWICZ, Stylist: Suzanne Shaker (right)

© WILLIAM ABRANOWICZ: p. 24 right; Designer & Stylist: Suzanne Shaker: pp. 29, 31 right; Designer: Charles Bumgardner: p. 32; Designers: Mark Chandler & Charles Bumgardner: p. 33; Stylist: Suzanne Shaker: p. 35 left; Designer: Carmelo Pomodoro: p. 44 right; Designers: Charles Bumgardner & Malcolm Smith: pp. 47, 53; p. 65 left; Architecture: Lee Minder: pp. 29, 31 right, 32, 35, 47, 53

© FELICIANO: pp. 25, 28 left; Designer: Anthony Child: p. 61 left; pp. 64, 65 right

© TRIA GIOVAN: Designer: Anna Thomas: pp. 2, 23; Designer: Anita Calevo: p. 28 right; Designer: Cathy Cook: p. 52 bottom; Designer: Charles Riley: pp. 68, 69 both

© MICK HALES: Designer: Jackye Lanham: pp. 45, 51 left

HEDRICH BLESSING: © Jim Hedrich: Designer: David Snyder: p. 31 top

© image/DENNIS KRUKOWSKI: Designer: Tonin MacCallum ASID, Inc.: p. 7; Designer: Robert E. Tartarini: p. 37; Designer: Samuel Botero Asssociates, Inc.: p. 39; Designer: M. H. Gomez Associates, Inc.: p. 63

© DAVID LIVINGSTON: Designer: Diane Chapman: p. 40 right; Designer: Paul Wiseman/Wiseman Group: p. 48 right; Designer: Sharon Campbell: p. 51 right; Designer: Cathleen Schmidtknecht: p. 60; Designer: Sue Fisher King: p. 66 left

© MICHAEL MUNDY: pp. 52 top, 55, 57, 58 right

© ERIC ROTH: Designer: Clara Hayes Barrett: p. 24 left; Designer: Richard Eustice: p. 27; Designer: Carole Kaplan: p. 30; Designer: Malibar Grove: p. 36 left; Designer: Janet Brown: p. 36 right; Designer: Joseph W. Drohan Associates Inc.: p. 40 left, p. 43; Designer: Mimi Packman: p. 54 left; Designer: Greg Cann/Cann & Co.: p. 58 left; Designer: Ida Goldstein/Interior Design Applications: p. 61 right; Designers: Isabelle & Alan Smiles/The Pomegranate Inn: p. 62

© BILL ROTHSCHILD: Designer: Lisette Mermod/Bloomingdales: p. 44 left; Designer: Richard Gruber: p. 49; Designer: Courtesy, Pierre Deux: p. 50; Designer: Ken Hockin: p. 59

© TIM STREET-PORTER: Designer: Penny Bianchi: pp. 6, 67; Designer: Simpson House: p. 22; Designer: Robert Woolf: p. 26; Designer: Brian Murphy: p. 34; Designer: Debra Jones: p. 35 right; Designers: Bob & Isabel Higgins: pp. 38–39; Location: Amanusa Hotel, Bali: p. 41; Designer: Hutton Wilkinson: p. 42; Location: Auberge du Soleil: p. 48 left; Designer: Barbara Barry: p. 54 right; Designer: Tom Calloway: p. 56